What's On Your Plate?

What's On Your Plate?

Norah Smaridge

**Illustrated by
C. Imbior Kudrna**

Abingdon
Nashville

What's On Your Plate?

Library of Congress Cataloging in Publication Data

SMARIDGE, NORAH.
    What's on your plate?
    Summary: Warns children about the ill effects of a "junk food"
diet and emphasizes the importance of good nutrition.
    1. Nutrition—Juvenile literature. 2. Diet—Juvenile literature.
3. Food, Junk—Juvenile literature. [1. Nutrition. 2. Diet. 3. Food,
Junk]
    I. Kudrna, C. Imbior (Charlene Imbior), ill. II. Title.
    TX355.S637   641.1   81-17684   AACR2

ISBN 0-687-44911-1

Manufactured in the United States of America

For my
Young friend,
Frederick Lange, Jr.

Food is a MOST important stuff.
So boys and girls must eat enough
(But never, never OVEReat
And grow too heavy for their feet).

There's food for cats and dogs and fish
(You wouldn't care to share their dish);
And food for cows and food for hens,
Who live on farms, in barns and pens.

There's special food for kangaroos,
Elephants, lions, caribous,
(No one will serve this food to YOU,
Unless you're living in the zoo).

There's PEOPLE FOOD, like cheese and meat,
But some of it is much too sweet,
And some is JUNK. It tastes delicious
But isn't in the least nutritious.

This little book will help a lot
To "show and tell" you what is what,
So you can choose the foods you should
That taste DEE-lish—and do you good!

What Have You Got to Lose?

Someday you may discover that
It isn't funny to be too fat.
You can't leap high to catch a ball;
You never win a race at all
(Unless it's with a turtle, who
Is twenty times as slow as you).

Be smart and do not hesitate,
But start right now to lose some weight—
Forget you love those candy bars,
And wave goodbye to cooky jars,

And ab-so-lute-ly turn your back
On cake and cookies for a snack.
Pretend that the refrigerator
Contains a real, live alligator
Ready to BITE you, if you try
To sneak a slice of chocolate pie!
(When hungry, you can always fix
A plate of fruit or carrot sticks.)

You'll find that when you're eating right,
You'll have a smaller appetite,
And in a month (or maybe two),
There'll be a whole lot less of YOU.

Wake Up and EAT!

Some girls and boys are sleepyheads;
You have to drag them from their beds.
They give their face and hands a lick
And whine that breakfast makes them SICK.
They push their cereal bowls away.
"It's not the proper kind!" they say.
"It doesn't POP. It doesn't PUFF.
Besides, it isn't SWEET enough!"
Their toast, they smuggle to the pup;
At juice, they turn their noses up;
And everybody has to beg
To make them eat their scrambled egg.

In school, they simply sit and scowl;
Their empty tummies start to growl;
They yawn so much, it's plain to see
They haven't ANY energy.
Long before lunch, they are, of course,
Hungry enough to eat a horse.
But in their weak and starving state,
They have to wait—and wait—and WAIT.

For kids like these, we have a tip—
Breakfast is NOT a meal to skip.

Junk Food—Who Needs It?

Suppose your daddy handed you
A beat-up rubber tire to chew?
Or Mother made you toasted snacks
Of rusty nails and crooked tacks?
Suppose your grandma baked a cake
And flavored it with broken rake?
Or boiled some junk to make a stew—
You'd think it CRAZY, wouldn't you?

Yet children throw their dimes away
On JUNK FOOD every single day—

Candies and drinks and chips and things—
With artificial flavorings
And artificial colors, too.
Those foods are only kidding you!
They don't do any good at all!
They never help to make you tall
Or give you thick and shining hair
Or big strong muscles everywhere
Or nice clear skin (a pleasant sight)
Or strong white teeth that really bite.

So leave those junk foods on the shelf,
Unless you LOVE to kid yourself.

Energy Tip

If all you want to do is SIT,
And yawn and scratch your head a bit,
Twiddle your thumbs, and drag your feet,
It doesn't matter WHAT you eat.
You can munch cookies, cake, and candy,
Keep sweet drinks and colas handy,
Sit on a cushion, soft and plump,
And grow into a BIG FAT LUMP.

But if you think it's lots of fun
To climb and jump and skate and run
And fly a kite and sail a boat
And dive and swim (instead of float),
Why THEN, you'll certainly agree
You have to EAT FOR ENERGY.

Junk food is OUT! Instead, you'll eat
Chicken and fish and eggs and meat,
And you'll be careful to include
Some FIBER in your daily food.
There's lots in fruit, and even more
In vegetables, cooked or raw—
In cereals too, like wheat and bran—
So learn to love them. (Yes, you can!)

Then you'll grow up with energy
Enough to swim across a sea
Or navigate a big balloon
Or ride a rocket to the moon
Or climb a peak or catch a whale
Or walk a tiger by his tail.

Such energy, we think—Don't you?—
Is well worth looking forward to.

Stay the Way You Are

Some kids are NATURALLY big,
Which doesn't mean they're FAT;
They have big bones and hands and feet,
But tummies that are flat.

BIG kids need lots of wholesome food
To keep them in repair;
They also need the right amount
Of exercise and air.

They should NOT lose a lot of weight—
They'd only get some laughs.
They'd grow so long and lean, they'd look
Exactly like giraffes!

Some kids are NATURALLY small,
Which doesn't mean they're THIN;
They have small frames, with small strong bones,
All neatly fitted in.

Those kids DON'T need to put on weight;
They're padded just enough.
They don't need second helpings
Or big plates of starchy stuff.

They should NOT try to fatten up,
For then there'd be a chance
Of other kids mistaking them
For baby elephants!

Get Going!

The yummyest meals will not taste right
Unless you have an appetite,
So when it's getting time to eat,
Don't make a face or drag your feet.

Instead, do something really bright
To give yourself an appetite.

Race a tiger
For a mile,
Wrestle with
A crocodile,
Take a hippo for a ride
All around the countryside,
Leapfrog with
A kangaroo,
Give a lion
A shampoo.

If you find this hard to do,
There are simpler methods, too.
Any one of them is right
For giving you an appetite.

Sweep the kitchen,
Mop the floor,
Run an errand
To the store,
Dump the garbage,
Shake the mat,
Brush the dog, or
Comb the cat.

When you're through, we guarantee
You'll wait for supper hungrily,
And even if it's stuff you hate,
You'll eat it all—You'll clean the plate!

What's THIS?

It's VERY rude to cry, "What's THIS?"
When someone serves a bowl
Of funny-looking soupy stuff,
Or else a casserole.
You can't decide what's in it
(There's cheese on top, and more).
You think you sniff some onion,
But you're not exactly sure.
That white stuff might be turnip
(Of course you'll fish it out).
And here's a carrot (much too small
To make a fuss about).

Is this the beef (or was it pork?)
You had last Sunday night?
It's cut in little pieces now;
You hope it tastes all right.

Leftovers TEEM with vitamins
And nutrients—and THAT
Is why you'd make a big mistake
To feed them to the cat.

Salad Stuff

Salad is such a healthful food—
It makes good sense to eat some daily.
Even a just-beginning cook
Can toss a salad fast and gaily.

When Susan makes a salad snack,
She doesn't use a lot of stuff—
Just lettuce and tomatoes (sliced)
Our Susan thinks is quite enough.

When Sammy makes a salad, though,
It's big enough to make you blink.
It looks as if he tosses in
Everything but the kitchen sink!

Celery, lettuce, chicory,
And baby carrots (chopped or whole),
Cucumber, radish, escarole.
Our Sammy throws into the bowl
Onions and olives—parsley too—
And bits of pepper on the top,
Until his mother loudly shouts,
"That's quite enough, dear! Sammy, STOP!"

Well, YOU can do the same as Sam
Or be content to copy Sue.
It doesn't matter what you use,
For ALL those things are good for you.
(But always wash EXTREMELY well
Whatever greens you use for filler—
Because a salad DOESN'T need
A big, fat, juicy caterpillar!)

Good for Bones

Slipping and sliding, falling flat,
Or tripping over stones—
Even the smartest kids, it seems,
Are always breaking bones.
Now, girls or boys would hate to break
The only bones they've got.
So if you long for good strong bones,
Eat yogurt (quite a lot).

Just spoon it from its little cup,
Or mix it with ripe red cherries,
Or pour it onto applesauce
Or any kind of berries.
(But if a BEAR is chasing you,
Which means you must be quick,
The handiest snack of all to grab
Is yogurt on a stick.)

Don't Touch!

Unless you're certain what they are,
Look most suspiciously
On berries growing on a bush,
A creeper, or a tree.
They're liable to be POISONOUS
And make you very sick;
So if you eat one by mistake,
Go tell a grown-up—QUICK!

Berries are tasty food for birds,
But birds are not like YOU.
They eat strange things, like bugs and worms,
Which people never do.

Unless you'd like your tummy pumped,
Just heed these warning words
And leave those berries on the bush—
They're strictly for the birds!

Hey Mom! No Cavities!

Timothy's in the dentist's chair!—
He says he's nice and cozy there.
He says he hopes the dentist will
Find lots of cavities to fill.
He says it gives him satisfaction
To have a great big tooth ex-trac-tion.
He says it never hurts a bit—
Well, don't believe a word of it!

Although the dentist GENTLY pokes
(And even tells you funny jokes),
You'd rather sit down ANYWHERE
Than in that huge and scary chair!

So, boys and girls, be smart enough
To say "Buzz off!" to starchy stuff
And food or drink that's supersweet.
(Just have it for a special treat.)

Then you will never need to fear
Your dental checkup twice a year.

Head Start

It's always fine to have a lot
Of hair upon your head
(Or maybe on your manly jaw
Or on your chin instead).

When boys grow up, they may decide
That they would really like
To have a little pointy beard
(The kind that's called Vandyke).

And some will grow a neat moustache.
(The toothbrush kind is small,
But if it isn't thick and dark,
It won't show up at all.)

Timothy wants a long white beard,
So when he goes outdoors,
People will smile at him and shout,
"Hello there, Santa Claus!"

On girls, of course, a bushy beard
Might look a little strange
(Nor would they really like to grow
Moustaches for a change).

Some girls will find a cap of curls
Is pleasing to their taste,
While some may like straight hair, or waves
That ripple to their waist.

You need to feed your head of hair
Right now, while you are small,
Or when you're grown, you might end up
With almost none at all!

Lucky you—most foods provide
Nutrition for your hair—
The only thing you need to do
Is eat your proper share.

So don't turn up your little nose
At any kind of dish
Of meat or chicken, beans or rice,
Fruit, vegetables, fish.

And even if you think it's stuff
That only RABBITS eat,
Remember—When you're growing hair,
SPINACH is hard to beat!

YUMMY!

Nothing makes your tastebuds flutter
Like mouth-watering peanut butter!
Sundays, weekdays, holidays—
You can serve it lots of ways.

When you have a growly belly,
Make a sandwich (mix with jelly).
Sometimes eat it like a dip,
With a carrot as a chip.
If you long for something nice,
Spread it on an apple slice.
(Try it on banana, too—
Almost any fruit will do.)

Ask your darling Gran to bake
A golden peanut-butter cake—
Cookies, too. They're both delicious!
(Tell her that they're MOST nutritious.)

When the game of baseball ends,
Serve on crackers to your friends.
(Also ask the kitten if
She would like a little sniff.)

If you've only got a minute,
You can stick you finger in it.
(But don't lick it from the jar—
You know how most mothers are!)